BUILD BACK BETTER SECTOR GUIDES
VOLUME 3: WATER, SANITATION, AND HYGIENE (WASH)

OCTOBER 2024

ASIAN DEVELOPMENT BANK

CONTENTS

TABLES, FIGURE, AND BOXES

ACKNOWLEDGMENTS

Preparation of this *Build Back Better Sector Guides* series was led by Belinda Hewitt, senior disaster risk management specialist, Climate Change and Sustainable Development Department (CCSD), ADB with substantive inputs and review from Brigitte Balthasar, senior disaster and climate risk financing specialist, CCSD, ADB; Charlotte Benson, former principal disaster risk management Specialist, ADB; Alexandra Galperin, unit head, disaster risk management, CCSD, ADB; Steven Goldfinch, senior disaster risk management specialist, CCSD, ADB; Anne Orquiza, senior disaster risk management officer, CCSD, ADB; Grendel Saldevar, senior operations assistant, CCSD, ADB; and Mario Unterwaining, former disaster risk management specialist (resilient infrastructure), ADB. The series was developed in close collaboration with ADB Sectors Group and country teams. Margie Peters-Fawcett copy edited the volumes with the assistance of Cherry Lynn Zafaralla as proofreader. Layout was created by Rommel Marilla, page proofs checking by Levi Rodolfo Lusterio, and administrative support by Michelle Imperial.

This volume was written by Eleanor Earl, Martin Findlay, Hayley Gryc, and Vita Sanderson of Arup and Mario Unterwainig, with inputs from Christian Walder, former urban development specialist, Sectors Group, ADB. Peer review by Thomas Fergusson of Miyamoto International is greatly appreciated.

ABBREVIATIONS

ADB	Asian Development Bank
BBB	build back better
DMC	developing member country
EAL	Emergency Assistance Loan
O&M	operation and maintenance
PDNA	post-disaster needs assessment
WASH	water, sanitation, and hygiene

ADB Indonesia: Community Water Services and Health Project (34152-013). For centuries, carrying bucket loads of water from well to home has fallen on the shoulders of the village's women. In the wake of the 2004 Indian Ocean tsunami and 2005 Nias earthquake, ADB provided over $20 million for the construction and rehabilitation of water and sanitation services in 400 villages in Nias and Aceh. Onohondro village received six clean water taps—one for every 50 families in the village.

Typhoon Ketsana (Ondoy) dropped 455 mm (17.9 in) of rain on Metro Manila in a span of 24 hours on 26 September 2009. A month's worth of rainfall in a single day washed away homes and flooded large areas, affecting thousands in the city and hampering access to basic services.

INTRODUCTION

Timely support for recovery and reconstruction efforts is critical when a disaster occurs to minimize any potential long-term setbacks to sustainable and inclusive socioeconomic development. It is essential to provide a window of opportunity to rebuild assets and improve livelihoods to increase climate and disaster resilience and reduce the risk of future hazards. With impacts of disasters projected to rise in the coming decades, affected by climate change, unplanned urbanization, poor risk governance, and a range of other trends, challenges relating to climate uncertainty, growing complexity of infrastructure systems, and the compounding nature of multiple hazard events underline the importance of ensuring that communities and infrastructure systems are equipped to cope, adapt, and recover when faced with future shocks and stresses.

Developing member countries (DMCs) of the Asian Development Bank (ADB) bear a disproportionate share of impacts from geophysical and extreme weather hazard events. Between 2004 and 2023, these DMCs accounted for 55% of global disaster fatalities and 74% of people affected.[1] Over this 20-year period, ADB has provided more than $9.1 billion in financing for emergency assistance loan (EAL) projects relating to disasters triggered by natural hazards, conflict, displacement, food insecurity, and health emergencies. The support that ADB offers its DMCs aims at ensuring resilient post-disaster recovery, as well as strengthening long-term disaster risk reduction (DRR).

ADB's Strategy 2030[2] and 2021 Disaster and Emergency Assistance Policy[3] outline commitments to ensure effective response and support to build back better (BBB) after a disaster or emergency.[4] Build back better refers to the use of the early recovery and reconstruction phases after a disaster or emergency to increase resilience of nations and communities to future events by integrating risk reduction

---

[1] Centre for Research on the Epidemiology of Disasters, EM-DAT: The International Disaster Database. www.emdat.be (accessed 5 February 2024). People affected by multiple disasters have been counted multiple times.

[2] ADB. 2017. *Strategy 2030: Achieving a Prosperous, Inclusive, Resilient, and Sustainable Asia and the Pacific*.

[3] ADB. 2021. *Revised Disaster and Emergency Assistance Policy*.

[4] Strategy 2030 sets out a commitment to "provide assistance for disaster response, including support to build back better."

measures into the restoration of physical infrastructure, societal systems, livelihoods, economies, and the environment.[5] By systematically promoting risk-informed, well-designed, and timely recovery and reconstruction, ADB supports the implementation of international agreements, such as the Sendai Framework for Disaster Risk Reduction 2015–2030 and the 2030 Agenda for Sustainable Development Goals, including its 17 Sustainable Development Goals, both of which promote a comprehensive approach toward disaster risk management (DRM) and BBB frameworks, including through community-based applications.

The six volumes that comprise the *Build Back Better Sector Guides* series aim to support ADB staff, consultants, and DMC counterparts to enhance the climate and disaster resilience of DMC communities, infrastructure, and systems through effective and well-designed post-disaster assistance. The volumes are based on principles, measures, and lessons learned from the international BBB literature; a review of over 40 ADB EALs processed between 2004 and 2021; and the outcome of consultations with a wide range of ADB staff.

Each of the volumes has been co-developed with relevant ADB sector and thematic groups. The sectors are areas in which ADB has played a key role in post-disaster recovery and reconstruction and where majority of ADB's disaster and emergency assistance has focused in the last 20 years. They are as follows:

(i)   Volume 1: Overview
(ii)   Volume 2: Transport
(iii)   Volume 3: Water, Sanitation, and Hygiene (WASH)
(iv)   Volume 4: Irrigated Agriculture
(v)   Volume 5: Social Infrastructure
(vi)   Volume 6: Power

This Volume 3 (Water, Sanitation, and Hygiene) provides an overview of good practice solutions, as well as considerations and lessons learned for building back better in the WASH sector but does not represent a general or step-by-step handbook on methods to prepare and implement post-disaster needs assessment (PDNA) or EALs; nor does it for other forms of post-disaster assistance.

The scope of this series includes building resilience in response to disasters triggered by natural hazards; however, some of its content is relevant to the broader aspect of economic recovery, including within the context of health emergencies and conflict. Complementary objectives, including equity and inclusion, green recovery, poverty reduction, and broader sustainable development, are also presented.

---

[5]   Adapted from United Nations General Assembly. 2016. Report of the Open-Ended Intergovernmental Expert Working Group on Indicators and Terminology Relating to DRR. Seventy-First Session, Item 19(c).

ADB's Role in Resilient Post-Disaster Recovery and Reconstruction

Following a disaster, ADB can mobilize rapid post-disaster technical support under the second window of its Asia Pacific Disaster Response Fund in areas such as the preparation of PDNAs; government-led recovery plans; and post-disaster projects, including emergency assistance loans. The post-disaster needs assessment is a well-established tailored methodology that is used for analyzing damage, loss, and needs prioritization. While the exercise should be led by the government, it is often conducted with the support of one or more international partners. The PDNA compiles information relating to the physical impacts of a disaster, economic value of damages and losses, human and macroeconomic impacts, and cost of early and long-term recovery needs and priorities. As such, the PDNA is an important tool to inform implementation of BBB through post-disaster programming.

Once recovery and reconstruction requirements have been assessed, ADB can mobilize finance for recovery and reconstruction through EALs, additional financing for pre-established projects, and investment projects that support longer-term reconstruction needs. ADB's 2021 Emergency Assistance Loan Policy enables the rapid approval of loans (within 12 weeks) to assist in the rebuilding of high-priority physical assets and the restoration of economic, social, and governance activities following disasters triggered by natural hazards, health emergencies, food insecurity, technological and industrial accidents, and post-conflict situations.[6] The Emergency Assistance Loan Policy and the 2021 Disaster and Emergency Assistance Policy aim to support DMC's BBB efforts to enhance climate and disaster resilience. Table 1 provides a list of additional resources relating to ADB's policies and directives relating to post-disaster assistance.

Table 1: Key Documents on ADB Policies and Guidance for Post-Disaster Assistance

Document	Web Page
2021 Disaster and Emergency Assistance Policy	http:// www.adb.org/documents/revised-disaster-and-emergency-assistance-policy
Revised Emergency Assistance Loan Policy	http:// www.adb.org/documents/revised-emergency-assistance-loan-policy
Establishment of a Second Window of Assistance under the Asia Pacific Disaster Response Fund	http:// www.adb.org/documents/establishment-second-window-assistance-under-asia-pacific-disaster-response-fund
Post-Disaster Needs Assessment Guidelines	http:// www.recoveryplatform.org/pdna
Disaster Recovery Planning: Explanatory Note and Case Study	https://www.adb.org/publications/disaster-recovery-planning-explanatory-note-case-study

Source: Asian Development Bank.

---

6   ADB. 2021. *Revised Emergency Assistance Loan Policy*.

Importance of Long-Term Resilience Building

Long-term and upstream approaches to resilience building are critical to minimize the impacts of disasters and ensure more effective and efficient use of post-disaster assistance resources. ADB can play a key role in leveraging increased risk awareness to ensure resilience-focused upstream planning. Where risk-responsive socioeconomic development and sector plans are already in place ahead of a disaster, they can more effectively guide long-term disaster recovery and bring about a shift toward resilience and sustainable development.

Risk-informed sector plans enable more rapid and effective post-disaster recovery and reconstruction where they are informed by comprehensive multihazard disaster risk assessments and incorporate ex ante recovery planning. Past ADB EALs, such as the 2015 Nepal: Earthquake Emergency Assistance Project (see Volume 5: Social Infrastructure) and the 2018 Tonga: Cyclone Gita Recovery Project (see Volume 6: Power), aligned recovery planning with climate and disaster resilience objectives set out in existing sector programs, government road maps, and the national development plan.

Use of the Build Back Better Sector Guides

This volume is intended to be read in combination with the introductory *Build Back Better Sector Guides—Volume 1: Overview*. The overview guide covers the broad measures that are likely relevant to any post-disaster recovery and reconstruction project, regardless of sector.

While this volume does not provide detailed technical guidance, it does provide various additional technical resources that can guide project-specific decision-making (Appendix: Suggested Readings). For any given project, it is important that resilience measures are selected appropriately and on a project-by-project basis, informed by an understanding of the specific WASH project components and local context. There should be analysis of current and future risk; economic development objectives; economic feasibility and viability; as well as relevant policies, including climate and disaster risk management and safeguards requirements.

ADB Pakistan: National Disaster Risk Management Fund (50316-001). Boy refreshing himself from the heat at a community water in Jhelum City in May 2018. The Flood Emergency Reconstruction and Resilience Project is part of the National Disaster Risk Management Fund and aims to provide safety to the people of Jhelum City and the surrounding localities and villages from the floods.

ADB India: Kolkata Environmental Improvement Investment Program - Tranche 1 (42266-023). Children play and fetch water from the community tap at the Behala slum area in Kolkata, India. The project included a range of resilience measures including early warning systems and enhanced sanitation to address recurring flood impacts.

II

DISASTER IMPACTS AND RECOVERY OBJECTIVES

It is critical to ensure the safe management of and access to WASH services during the recovery phase of a disaster to ensure human safety and health and to minimize any secondary impact on community lives and well-being. Given that access to safely managed water and sanitation services is a human right, restoration and provision of WASH services following a disaster often has accelerated, phased, and complex programming requirements.

Like infrastructure, WASH services are exposed to hazards due to their broad spatial distribution and reliance on natural systems, including groundwater and surface water sources. Natural hazard impacts on water and sanitation resources can significantly influence the quality, quantity, and accessibility of WASH, post-disaster. Extreme weather events can cause water contamination, water scarcity, and/or flooding. Deterioration and damage to WASH systems following a disaster can proliferate the spread of water-related diseases such as cholera, acute watery diarrhea, and typhoid; and perpetuate the spread of vector-borne disease like malaria and dengue fever, in some cases leading to a secondary health emergency. The impact on services is likely to be experienced differently between urban and rural areas, since rural communities often rely on decentralized as well as on-site systems. Where natural hazard events occur in urban settings, additional factors may include larger, and more complex WASH systems, population concentration and displacement.

In many parts of Asia and the Pacific, climate change is placing additional pressure on scarce water resources, thus perpetuating fragility of WASH systems. Globally, 2 billion people currently lack access to reliable WASH services let alone resilient WASH infrastructure, with 1.2 billion devoid of even the basic of sanitation services,[7] thus making them more vulnerable to disaster impacts.[8] Post-disaster Improvements to WASH services, therefore, should

---

[7] WHO and UNICEF. 2021. *Progress on Household Drinking Water, Sanitation and Hygiene 2000–2020: Five Years into the SDGs*. World Health Organization and United Nations Children's Fund.

[8] Global WASH Cluster. 2011. *Disaster Risk Reduction and Water, Sanitation and Hygiene: Comprehensive Guidance*.

aim to help communities achieve the United Nations targets for Sustainable Development Goal 6 ("universal and equitable access to safe and affordable drinking water for all") by 2030. By doing so, WASH can be termed as a "no regrets" expenditure during reconstruction.

Resilient WASH infrastructure cannot be considered without also considering the entire water system, including the catchment[9] and its interdependency with other sectors. For example, if water is needed for a hygiene facility, adequate management of surface water is necessary to ensure the quantity and quality of water from the facility's outlet. WASH systems are critical in the recovery of other infrastructure and social sectors, such as energy, food, and resumption of services such as health care and education.

Table 2 lists examples from PDNAs relating to events during the past in Asia and the Pacific, including WASH sector damage and loss. Broader BBB objectives in addition to building climate and disaster resilience are shown in Box 1.

Table 2: Examples of Water Sector Disaster Effects and Recovery Needs

Event	Disaster Effects (Damage and Loss) ($ million)[a]		Recovery Needs ($ million)[b]	
	Infrastructure[b]	Water	Infrastructure[b]	Water
Earthquake (Nepal), 2015[c]	652	111 (17%)	743	181 (24%)
Cyclone Winston (Fiji), 2016[d]	119	12 (10%)	136	12 (9%)
Floods and landslides (Sri Lanka), 2017[e]	103	11 (11%)	170	56 (33%)
Floods (Lao People's Democratic Republic), 2018[f]	219	8.33 (4%)	290	(3%)

[a] Where the required value is not available, amounts in local currency are converted to United States dollars based on the exchange rate for the event year, and sourced from World Bank Development Indicators (accessed 1 June 2023).

[b] Infrastructure damage and loss is defined based on the post-disaster needs assessment guidelines produced by the Global Fund for Disaster Reconstruction and Recovery (GFDRR. 2013. *Post-Disaster Needs Assessments: Guidelines—Volume A*). These guidelines include the sectors of water and sanitation, community infrastructure, energy, transport, and telecommunications.

[c] Government of Nepal. 2015. *Nepal Earthquake 2015: Post Disaster Needs Assessment—Volume A: Key Findings*. National Planning Commission

[d] Government of Fiji. 2016. Post-Disaster Needs Assessment Tropical Cyclone Winston. 20 February.

[e] Government of Sri Lanka. 2017. Sri Lanka Rapid Post Disaster Needs Assessment: Floods and Landslides. Ministry of National Policies and Economic Affairs and Ministry of Disaster Management.

[f] Government of the Lao People's Democratic Republic. 2018. *Post-Disaster Needs Assessment 2018 Floods, Lao PDR*.

Source: Asian Development Bank.

---

[9]   Area collecting water that drains to a particular river or reservoir, also referred to as a watershed or drainage basin.

> ### Box 1: Key Objectives for Post-Disaster Recovery and Reconstruction of Water, Sanitation, and Hygiene
>
> Global best practice studies and lessons learned in Asian Development Bank (ADB) projects suggest that in addition to building climate and disaster resilience, key post-disaster recovery and reconstruction objectives for water, sanitation, and hygiene (WASH) systems should include the following:
>
> - Provide **safe, equitable, and affordable access** to WASH services for all to improve health and living standards, with special attention to the needs of the poorest groups, women, children, older people, and those with disabilities.
> - Adopt and maintain **sustainable and adaptable solutions** that promote decarbonization and broader environmental benefit, such as nature-based water management systems and renewable energy-driven WASH services.
> - Reduce the **impacts on connected infrastructure,** including energy and transport. For example, poorly designed or managed WASH systems may disrupt buried electrical cabling or damage roads.
> - Adopt **new technology and innovation** once better outcomes are reached, such as the use of sensors to monitor WASH infrastructure.
> - Establish **new value chains** to support new climate and disaster-resilient pathways. For example, fecal sludge (i.e., material from on-site sanitation systems) is high in nutrients once appropriately treated as it has a potential for the generation of fertilizer, fuel, and animal feed, thus contributing to a circular economy.
>
> The World Health Organization estimates that for every dollar invested in water and sanitation, there is a four-fold return in the cost of health care for each individual and therefore society as a whole.[a]
>
> ---
>
> [a] United Nations. 2014. Every Dollar Invested in Water, Sanitation Brings Four-Fold Return in Costs: UN. *UN News.* 19 November.
>
> Source: Asian Development Bank.

ADB Bangladesh: Participatory Small-Scale Water Resources Sector Project (39432-013). The project includes support to strengthen the capability of agencies overseeing the sector, and developing water management cooperative associations that will undertake the day-to-day operations of small-scale water services.

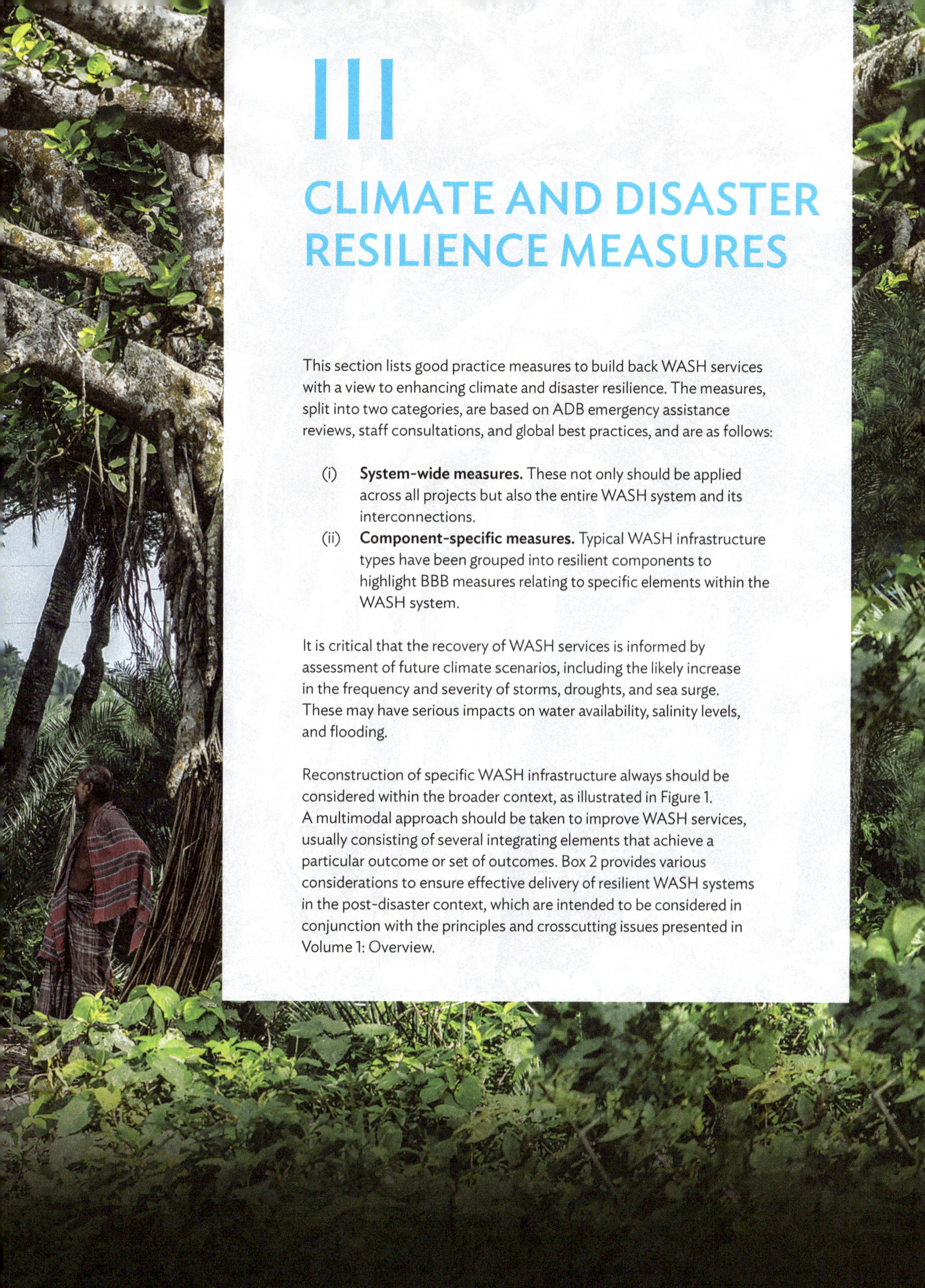

III

CLIMATE AND DISASTER RESILIENCE MEASURES

This section lists good practice measures to build back WASH services with a view to enhancing climate and disaster resilience. The measures, split into two categories, are based on ADB emergency assistance reviews, staff consultations, and global best practices, and are as follows:

(i)   **System-wide measures.** These not only should be applied across all projects but also the entire WASH system and its interconnections.

(ii) **Component-specific measures.** Typical WASH infrastructure types have been grouped into resilient components to highlight BBB measures relating to specific elements within the WASH system.

It is critical that the recovery of WASH services is informed by assessment of future climate scenarios, including the likely increase in the frequency and severity of storms, droughts, and sea surge. These may have serious impacts on water availability, salinity levels, and flooding.

Reconstruction of specific WASH infrastructure always should be considered within the broader context, as illustrated in Figure 1. A multimodal approach should be taken to improve WASH services, usually consisting of several integrating elements that achieve a particular outcome or set of outcomes. Box 2 provides various considerations to ensure effective delivery of resilient WASH systems in the post-disaster context, which are intended to be considered in conjunction with the principles and crosscutting issues presented in Volume 1: Overview.

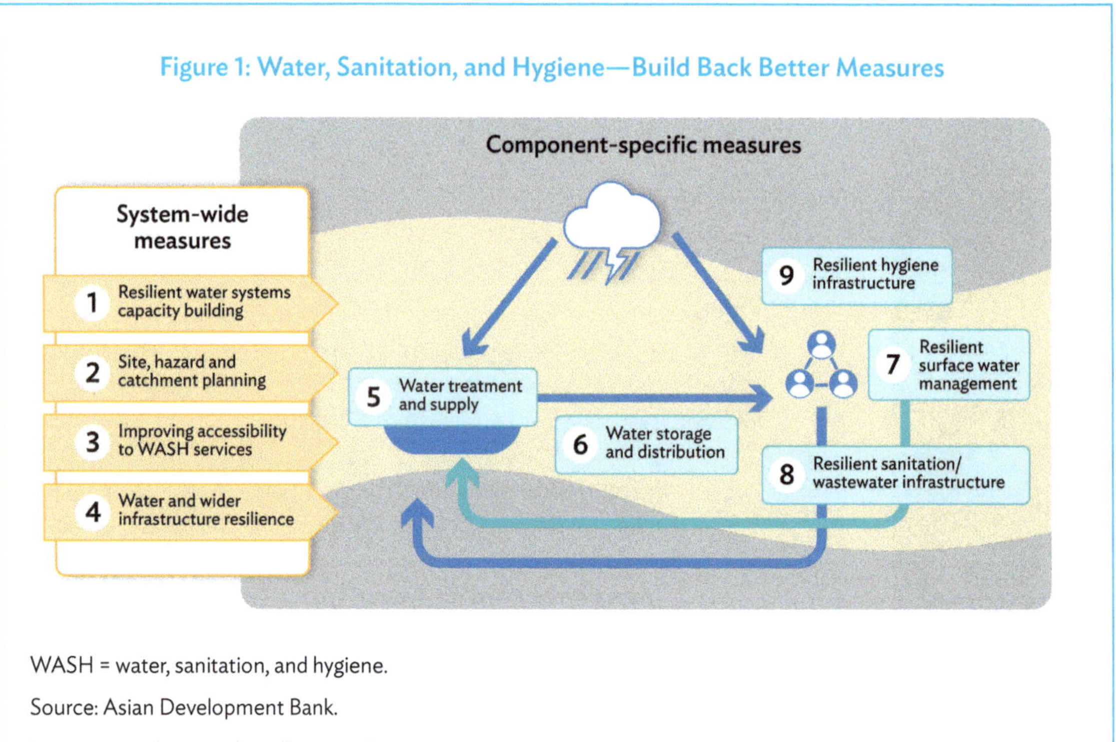

WASH = water, sanitation, and hygiene.

Source: Asian Development Bank.

Box 2: Considerations for the Delivery of Water, Sanitation, and Hygiene

The water, sanitation, and hygiene (WASH) sector programming following a disaster requires careful deliberation to ensure that objectives for climate and disaster resilience are implemented effectively, particularly in terms of the following sector considerations and constraints.

- **Challenges of phasing WASH programs.** The close coupling of human and natural systems means that phased WASH programs can be quite challenging, particularly in the face of post-disaster disruption. For example, rainfall cannot be prevented during reconstruction or when repairing drainage infrastructure. As such, thought must be given to careful phasing of temporary and long-term solutions and installing effective temporary infrastructure during restoration of existing systems.
- **Temporary "work-around" solutions.** These already may be in place when WASH reconstruction begins, given the obvious urgency. Work-around solutions such as temporary latrines should be either elevated and integrated into new WASH infrastructure design or replaced with permanent solutions.
- **Differentiated WASH requirements.** The cultural and religious beliefs of the effected populations should be carefully considered because WASH requirements vary from country to country. This can be particularly complex with regard to differentiated needs of local communities and displaced groups. For example, religious belief and/or cultural norms may require different menstrual hygiene facilities for women and girls. In some Muslim countries cleansing is performed using water (not paper) and washing before prayers (Wudu or Ablution) can significantly increase the water needs for the population being served.

Source: Asian Development Bank.

Water System Capacity Building

Resilient recovery and reconstruction primarily require ensuring a clear understanding of the WASH value chain, since it is unlikely that a country would have only one responsible stakeholder or institution to manage the entire system from the source of water to the wastewater treatment stage. For example, during recovery and reconstruction, the national government may be responsible for funding, policy making, and planning; the local government for stormwater drainage; and a water utility for construction and maintenance of the water supply and wastewater infrastructure. Therefore, appraisal of key stakeholders and opportunities to strengthen future resilience should be carried out following a disaster with participation from local staff and stakeholders, covering the following:

(i)   WASH infrastructure stakeholders and governance systems at the national, state, and local levels; water and energy utilities; and communities;
(ii)   relationship between stakeholders, including their respective governance structure(s);
(iii) identification of those responsible for the management and delivery of repairs and upgrades, emergency and contingency planning, day-to-day operation and maintenance (O&M) of individual WASH system components, and dissemination of information to affected communities to maintain accountability and better support the decision-making process;[10]
(iv)   potential funding mechanisms, including release of additional funds and resources following future hazard events;
(v)   WASH cluster or sector and relevant nongovernment organizations working in the geographic area; and
(vi)   identification of skills, gaps, and a potential WASH training plan that involves local stakeholders.

An example of a WASH system stakeholder analysis approach is provided in the resource list in Box 7. The assessment should be contextualized for each given WASH activity and project.

Usually, WASH services are located close to the community; this provides residents an opportunity to play a key role in reconstruction efforts, so long as there is sufficient capacity building and when it is culturally appropriate. Women, girls, and vulnerable groups should be included in the decision-making process by building their awareness and capacity to be prepared and enabling them to maintain WASH services in the event of future damage and disruption. Capacity building is necessary to make certain that hygiene provision is well understood, that safe water storage handling and practices are applied, and contingency supplies are accessible. Capacity building also includes O&M planning for reconstructed WASH infrastructure so that services, e.g., implementation of contingency planning measures into future WASH asset maintenance and water safety plans, are resilient and sustainable.

---

[10]   Global WASH Cluster. 2020. *Delivering Humanitarian WASH at Scale, Anywhere and Any Time, Road Map 2020–2025.* United Nations Children's Fund.

Site, Hazard, and Catchment Planning

A multihazard systems-level risk assessment of WASH infrastructure sites, delivered as part of recovery planning, can help to quantify and communicate differences between reconstruction options, including preferred locations and protective measures to minimize hazard exposure. For example, in a case where it is inconvenient for community access to construct a berm around a site to reduce flood risk, users and stakeholders may be more accepting if the risk reduction benefits are clearly communicated.

The site-specific multihazard risk assessment must consider the potential impacts from reconstruction work on water catchments as well as the risks posed to the WASH system. Ideally, regional catchment planning should be undertaken, including analyses of interconnected WASH systems upstream and downstream. Furthermore, early warning systems to improve risk management should be considered. Opportunities to increase distribution and diversity should be explored to reduce potential impacts of future natural hazard events on the WASH system.

Poorly designed or badly constructed WASH infrastructure can pose health risks to the community being served, and as such, any intervention should be carefully planned, designed, and executed with a reliable factor of safety and considering current and future climate and disaster risks. For example, latrine pits being excavated in a high-water table area during the dry season may well breach the water table during the rainy season and thus lead to a subsurface contamination issue that is hard to diagnose. Further to this, any existing WASH infrastructure should be carefully assessed directly after a disaster to ensure any damage is well understood and included as part of the rehabilitation works that take place during any BBB intervention.

Improving the Accessibility to WASH Services

The need for continued access to WASH services during disaster recovery is critical. Immediate repair rehabilitation and reconstruction of WASH services is therefore of utmost priority, particularly in public facilities such as schools, markets, and buildings. Facilities should be easily accessible, including in hazardous conditions such as high river flow.

Communities that are poor or those where people live on the margins, such as in floodplains, may be particularly vulnerable and prone to reduced access to WASH services. Post-disaster assistance in this case will provide an opening to increase flood resilience and improve access to services for these groups in a way that will improve the infrastructure, services, and land use.

Acceptance of any repaired, rehabilitated, or reconstructed WASH infrastructure will depend also on special attention to the needs of women, girls, and other vulnerable groups, particularly those involved in water-related tasks that are disrupted following a disaster, such as the daily collection of water. Given that some needs may not be well understood or considered by the wider community as taboo topics, for example, menstruation, it is essential to build a supportive environment wherein such groups are sensitively recognized and catered for. This can be achieved by performing key informant interviews and or focus group discussions that allow a safe and secure space for frank and useful discussion. If performed well this can enhance community buy-in and support successful interventions such as providing adequate infrastructure for good menstrual hygiene and creating places where one can change and bathe in a clean dignified and private space.[11]

Box 3: Water, Sanitation, and Hygiene Infrastructure Recovery to Reduce the Vulnerability of Women and Girls in Nepal

Following the 2015 Nepal earthquake, the destruction of critical water, sanitation, and hygiene infrastructure had a profound effect on the ability of women and men to engage in normal daily activities. Disruption of the water supply had a disproportionate negative effect on women and girls, in particular, who are traditionally responsible for most of household water management. The time it takes for them to fetch water increased by three hours in some of the affected areas. The destruction of toilets, compounded by lack of water, as well as poor living conditions that do not afford privacy to women and girls, seriously impacted the personal hygiene of women and adolescent girls. The Government of Nepal's National Planning Commission therefore constructed public and private toilets with proper lighting to provide them with privacy, a move that supported resiliency in recovery and reconstruction efforts while, at the same time, shifting to a model of universal access to water supply and sanitation services.

To ensure recovery efforts would be effective, the Ministry of Urban Development led and coordinated stakeholder consultations wherein roles and responsibilities, jurisdictions, and available resources were established; and implementation strategies, sectoral policy making, and institutional arrangements were agreed on. The implementation mechanism selected strengthened decentralization and capacity building efforts at the local level to ensure interventions were sustainable.

Sources: Adapted from Government of Nepal. 2015. *Nepal Earthquake 2015: Post Disaster Needs Assessment—Volume A: Key Findings.* National Planning Commission; and I. Rauniyar. 2019. *Nepal Four Years After: On a Path to Recovery. Prevention Web.* 30 April.

Integration of Water, Sanitation, and Hygiene into Wider Infrastructure Systems

Most infrastructure systems, such as social infrastructure, transport, industry, energy, food supply, livelihoods, health, and waste rely heavily on water supply and water defenses including coastal and river flood barriers. WASH systems, in turn, rely on various sectors for their safe and resilient performance, debatably to a greater extent than other sectors. Disruption to a WASH system due to disaster also has significant domino effects on other sectors like health care and agriculture.

Following disruption or damage, it is important to consider how the overall WASH system has performed previously—including whether there have been any cascading impacts across the wider infrastructure systems—to identify resilience solutions that improve integration, flexibility, and redundancy. Consideration should be given to decentralizing to improve resilience to future disasters

---

[11]   University of Leeds. 2022. *Incontinence and WASH Focusing on People in Humanitarian and Low- and Middle-Income Contexts.* Water, Sanitation and Health (WASH) Blog.

particularly in the presence of complex governance practices and geographic or resource constraints. Parallel systems such as biological reactors to treat and sterilize water can operate at minimum and maximum water flow, thereby allowing for better quality control of water, maintenance, and redundancy. Decentralized infrastructure in WASH systems such as off-grid power sources for pumps will help to ensure a continuous supply of water at times when disaster may affect the centralized power system, though trade-offs with potentially increased requirements for O&M and technical capacity need to be carefully considered.

Significant improvements to WASH system integration and resilience can be achieved by integrating secure digital technology into reconstruction projects. To be effective, however, digital systems must be made resilient so that manual control or direct device control from pumping valves, storm and blackwater storage or septic tanks, among others is possible as a backup in case of emergency (Table 3).

Table 3: Examples of Digital Technology for Resilient Water, Sanitation, and Hygiene System Recovery

Approach	Example
Backup systems	Backup systems for supervisory control and data acquisition may enable water, sanitation, and hygiene systems to continue operating following either human error or upon impact of a natural hazard.
Monitoring	Operational efficiency, as well as the quantification of climate and disaster impacts, can be achieved through sensors to monitor water, sanitation, and hygiene services. The use of smart remote and measuring devices for water level, water damage or leakage to infrastructure, and service performance will retrieve real-time conditions, particularly where recovery needs arising from a hazard need to be identified and prioritized.

Source: Asian Development Bank.

Resilient Water Supply and Treatment

Supply and treatment of water are considered post-disaster recovery priorities to ensure sufficient quantities of quality water to reduce the risk of disease outbreaks such as cholera, acute watery diarrhea, and skin infections such as scabies. Rebuilding or rehabilitating infrastructure offers the potential to upgrade water sources to the levels prescribed by the World Health Organization and the United Nations Children's Fund:[12] either "safely managed" or at least "basic."

---

[12]   Basic water sources include protected wells or boreholes and springs, where collection time is no more than 30 minutes round-trip from the premises, whereas safely managed sources are those that are available on the premises and free from fecal and chemical contamination. See World Health Organization (WHO) and UNICEF. 2022. *Joint Monitoring Program for Water Supply, Sanitation and Hygiene* (accessed 14 June 2024).

Independent raw water sources can help to compensate for climate and disaster impacts on the system that may affect the quality and quantity of water, as when groundwater levels or spring eyes change due to earthquake. Where culturally and climatically appropriate, rainwater harvesting may be promoted as part of reconstruction efforts to diversify the supply of water as a contingency against disruption of the main water supply, particularly to provide supplementary water for washing and livestock. Rainwater harvesting tanks must be sealed for safety and to prevent mosquito breeding. Increasing connections between drinking water sources in the distribution network and identifying multiple independent water sources ensures the network is readily adaptable in the event of damage to or disruption in a particular section. It is necessary, however, to ensure that there is continuous water supply and water exchange so that connections remain hygienic; for example, there should be no dead ends or legs in the pipework, and water flow should be continuous.

The sealing of wells or boreholes and protection of spring catchments during reconstruction and/or repair of damaged wells will help to prevent future flood water infiltration. Wells or boreholes should preferably be drilled rather than hand-dug at a level deeper than the previous well, considering drawdown and any seasonal variation to provide increased resilience to natural hazards such as drought or earthquakes, greater construction safety, and lower levels of contamination.

Good quality raw water sources should reduce water treatment costs and the likelihood of contamination during disasters. Although groundwater and spring water tend to be, in general, less contaminated than surface water, there nevertheless are areas where there is microbial or other contamination like arsenic, fluoride, or salinity in coastal areas. All raw water sources need to be evaluated for quality of the water prior to repair or reconstruction planning, and appropriate treatment provided prior to consumption. In addition, a hydrogeological survey before the drilling of new wells and boreholes will increase the likelihood of appropriate water quantity. Effort should be made to ensure that these sources are well protected against future contamination, particularly if there are other wide-scale reconstruction efforts taking place in the area.

Water treatment systems that call for repair or replacement should be sized with future needs in mind; they also should easily cater to future demand or the temporary influx of displaced populations. Residual chlorination should be considered to mitigate the risk of contamination throughout the water supply chain using storage tanks or pipes, or after collection. Tanks and connection points are most likely to be damaged in a hazard event; therefore, during reconstruction and repair, measures such as improving the robustness of selected materials should be put in place to improve resilience of these components.

Equally, BBB provides an important opportunity to enhance the quality, accessibility and diversity of water supply, especially for poor and vulnerable stakeholders. An example of BBB of a community water supply system is provided in Box 4.

Box 4: Project Example—CARE India Resilient Hand Pumps

In May 2009, a cyclone hit India's southeast coast affecting more than 6 million people and causing contamination of water sources with saline water. Surface water ponds, previously used for the supply of water, became saline and therefore unsafe for use.

CARE India carried out reconstruction of the water supply system. Given the high vulnerability of the community and its infrastructure to future flooding, new hand pumps were installed on raised platforms to ensure a continued supply of water in the event of inundation. Pumps were adapted to allow people with disabilities to easily access the infrastructure. The project included support for hardware, software, and community organization. User committees were formed and trained in the basic operation, maintenance, and administration of tasks, which are essential to keep the pumps operational in times of disaster, while community engagement, combined with a cost-recovery system, was instrumental in the sustainability of systems.

Source: Global WASH Cluster. 2011. Disaster Risk Reduction and Water, Sanitation and Hygiene: Comprehensive Guidance.

Resilient Water Storage and Distribution

Decentralizing drinking water storage and supply during reconstruction will ensure that the water system will be able to cope better in the event of future climate hazards and disasters, including during seasonal flow variability. Should disruption of the main water supply occur, there should be a sufficient water reserve. For example, where appropriate, many smaller volume storage tanks can be used or large water tanks may be segregated into separate, smaller storage chambers, and emergency shut-off valves employed to reduce system failure.

Flow control valves should be placed throughout the distribution system during repair, rehabilitation, or reconstruction to separate the network sections that have failed because of a disaster and allow for a phased approach to maintenance repair and rehabilitation. Gate valves tend to be more appropriate in this case due to their reduced upfront and maintenance costs.

Reconstruction and repair of the distribution system should seek to reduce consumption and nonrevenue water[13] to build resilience to future droughts and water insecurity. Loss of water can be reduced by simple interventions in the form of specification for durable materials when replacing storage tanks, pipes, and taps. Flow rate monitoring can be introduced to inform prompt interventions to reduce water loss from leakage, theft, or when damage occurs due to natural hazards.

---

[13]   Nonrevenue water is water that has been produced and is "lost" before it reaches the consumer. Losses can be real losses (through leaks, sometimes also referred to as physical losses) or apparent losses (through theft or metering inaccuracies).

Damaged pipes are a source of contamination; therefore, hazard-resistant pipe materials should be selected based on relevant natural hazards. For example, in areas of seismic risk, ductile iron pipes or PVC with flexible joints are recommended, among other similar types. Installing pipes above ground on thrust-blocks or burying and encasing pipes in concrete also can provide additional protection, depending on the local context.

Reconstructed water systems should be designed to flow by gravity, where possible, to reduce the risk of failure due to pump malfunction or lack of power during a disaster event, as well as to reduce maintenance demand and increase sustainability. Where pumping systems are required, the size should be of adequate capacity to operate during a disaster or high- and low-flow events, as well as to account for future growth demand.

Resilient Surface Water Management

Surface water often is made up of greywater and stormwater runoff and should be dealt with at source in the design of reconstruction schemes to benefit the wider catchment and local communities and reduce natural hazard risks including flood, erosion, and landslide. A climate and disaster risk assessment that includes hydrological and hydraulic modeling should inform the provision of adequate drainage and stormwater capacity during reconstruction to prevent the overflow of stormwater and damage during future extreme rainfall. Typical approaches for improving resilience can include a better design of valves, increased cross-sectional area of drainage conduits and flow capacity, and more effective stormwater culverts, while more sustainable measures can reduce and slow water flow at source.

Where, feasible, stormwater and greywater should be separated from sewerage systems. This will prevent fecal contamination of floodwater that will increase the risk of waterborne disease during extreme flood events.

Adopting integrated flood risk management measures and nature-based solutions to reconstructed rainwater storage may increase water absorption, improve water quality, and minimize flood risk.[14] Integrating measures such as green roofs, walls, and streets in the reconstruction of the wider infrastructure also will minimize water flow and increase storage capacity. Such approaches have significant co-benefits by reducing the urban heat island effect, improving air quality, and protecting groundwater. An example of an integrated approach taken in Sri Lanka is provided in Box 5.

Where, feasible, stormwater and greywater should be separated from sewerage systems. This will prevent fecal contamination of floodwater that will increase the risk of waterborne disease during extreme flood events.

---

[14]   ADB. 2019. *Strategy 2030 Operational Plan for Priority 3: Tackling Climate Change, Building Climate and Disaster Resilience, and Enhancing Environmental Sustainability, 2019–2024.*

Box 5: Project Example—Sri Lanka Surface Water Management

In 2005, Action Against Hunger (*Action Contre la Faim*) worked with communities impacted by the 2004 Indian Ocean earthquake and tsunami in Sri Lanka to deliver an integrated and sustainable systems project. Communities in the eastern towns of Batticaloa and Trincomalee were flooded by stagnant water that had been prevented from flowing away from sites due to an absence of drainage systems. Stagnant water surrounding the houses occur not only during extreme weather events but also post-event due to discharges from water, sanitation, and hygiene facilities, causing serious risk to community health and contributing to increased mosquitoes, contaminated water, and accumulated humidity on the ground floor of post-disaster shelters.

To build back better, the project designed and constructed a variety of sustainable drainage systems to reduce the risk of flood and improve site drainage. Trees, for example, were planted alongside new road corridors to reduce runoff water, protect the road from sun and rain, increase shade, and reduce pollution in the local community.

The project also developed a stormwater management guide that aims to inform and support other organizations operating in the area so that they too can support community drainage upgrades.

Source: C. Alaman and J. Zarins. 2005. Storm Drainage Guidelines in Transitional Accommodation Centres. ACF and Project Galle.

Resilient Sanitation and Wastewater Infrastructure

Wastewater and sanitation infrastructure are initial priorities for any recovery. Wastewater is often a mix of blackwater, greywater, and stormwater.[15] Ideally, these water types are dealt with separately to keep water at its highest quality and reduce the necessary resources for treatment.

The rebuilding or rehabilitating of latrines will open the door to not only install like-for-like replacements, but also to upgrade the sanitation infrastructure to the level of either safely managed or, at least, basic,[16] all of which will be a challenge to achieve. However, once the immediate needs of the population are met, improvements can be gradually introduced—often referred to as the "sanitation ladder."

Where wastewater treatment plants have been damaged by disasters, an assessment of current and future sources of wastewater should be made based on the future growth and decline of populations, and upgrades to the system made accordingly. In areas where decentralized sanitation options are common but not governed under a regulatory framework, it is possible to formalize these by engaging local legislators and wastewater treatment operators during the reconstruction period to prevent disease transmission and further environmental degradation in the long term.

---

[15] Blackwater refers to water contaminated with fecal matter; greywater, also known as sullage, is wastewater from baths, sinks, and washing that is not contaminated with fecal matter; and stormwater is water accumulated due to precipitation, including rainfall events.

[16] Basic services include ventilated and better pit latrines that are not shared with other households, whereas safely managed facilities refer to facilities where the waste is then treated in situ or offsite (i.e., a septic tank or sewerage system connected to a wastewater treatment plant). See WHO and UNICEF. 2022. Joint Monitoring Program for Water Supply, Sanitation and Hygiene Global Database (accessed 14 June 2024).

Essential wastewater structures—treatment plants, septic tanks, pump stations, pipework—should be sufficiently resilient to natural hazards. This includes accounting for soil stability, potential erosion and siltation of infrastructure foundations, and buoyancy loading from raised groundwater levels. Measures such as sealing septic tanks and installing nonreturn valves should be applied to protect against flooding, along with capacity building (Box 6).

Box 6: Project Example—Developing Flood-Resilient Sanitation Systems

In response to the Kerala flooding in India in 2018, the United Nations Children's Fund (UNICEF) worked with the local government to build the capacity of its institutions and strengthen wastewater treatment systems to reduce the likelihood in future events of fecal waste contamination of drinking water. Before 2018, Kerala had suffered from a lack of wastewater treatment plants, whereby untreated fecal sludge from septic tanks was dumped into local rivers. The health and environmental risks particularly water- and vector-borne diseases associated with this practice were exacerbated across the region, especially during actual flooding. To build back better following the floods, UNICEF extended its financial support and technical assistance to construct two fecal sludge treatment plants and pilot new sewage treatment plants in the worst affected districts of Kerala.

Source: UNICEF. 2020. Building Back Better: Kerala Addressing Post-Disaster Recovery Needs. *WASH Field Note.* FN/50/2020.

Resilient Hygiene Infrastructure

Hygiene infrastructure should be prioritized in any reconstruction and recovery effort by providing adequate hand washing facilities to prevent the spread of disease. Replacing like-for-like products should be complemented by upgraded hygiene infrastructure to at least a basic level.[17]

Post-disaster, infrastructure should be reconstructed with resilience and hygiene in mind. Simple solutions such as low-flow and foot-operated taps can be applied in urban and rural settings alike to minimize water use and secure availability of quality water.[18]

Early market engagement should take place to understand how the hygiene product value chain (includes soap, menstrual hygiene materials) can be made more resilient to climate and disaster risk. Where supply chains are at risk of disruption, local production of soap and other hygiene materials should be encouraged.

---

[17] Basic hand washing facilities are those that are available in the home with access to soap and water. See WHO and UNICEF. 2022. Joint Monitoring Program for Water Supply, Sanitation and Hygiene Global Database.

[18] J. Davis and R. Lambert. 2002. *Engineering in Emergencies: A Practical Guide for Relief Workers.* 2nd ed. Intermediate Technology Development Group.

SUGGESTED READINGS

The following technical and subject matter resources are further references in implementing nonstructural build back better measures.

ACF. 2013. *ACF-International Manual. 1 + 1 = 3. How to Integrate WASH and MHCP Activities for Better Humanitarian Projects.*

CAWST. 2022. Stakeholder Analysis Instructions.

Cities Alliance. 2021. *Building Climate Resilient and Sustainable Cities for All.*

J. Colin. 1999. *VLOM for Rural Water Supply: Lessons from Experience.* Water and Environmental Health at London and Loughborough.

A. Coerver et al. *Compendium of Water Supply Technologies in Emergencies.* German WASH Network and University of Applied Sciences and Arts.

M. Coultas, R. Iyer, and J. Myers. 2020. *Handwashing Compendium for Low Resource Settings: A Living Document.* 2nd ed. The Sanitation Learning Hub.

Global WASH Cluster. 2011. Disaster Risk Reduction and Water, Sanitation and Hygiene: Comprehensive Guidance.

E. Tilley et al. n.d. *Compendium of Sanitation Systems and Technologies.* 2nd revised ed. Water Supply and Collaborative Council.

Sphere. 2018. *The Sphere Handbook: Humanitarian Charter and Minimum Standards in Humanitarian Response.* 4th ed.

United Nations High Commissioner for Refugees. 2020. WASH Manual: Practical Guide for Refugee Settings. 7th ed.

United Nations Children's Fund (UNICEF). 2019. Global Framework for Urban Water, Sanitation and Hygiene: A Strategic Vision for Urban WASH Programming across Global, Regional and Country Levels.

UNICEF. 2019. Water, Sanitation and Hygiene: A Guidance Note for Leaving No One Behind.

UNICEF. 2020. Building Back Better: Kerala Addressing Post-Disaster Recovery Needs. *WASH Field Note.* FN/50/2020.

United Nations Children's Fund and Global Water Partnership. 2017. WASH Climate Resilient Development, Appraising and Prioritizing Options for Climate Resilient WASH.

United Nations Office for Project Services. 2024. Developing Inclusive Water, Sanitation and Hygiene Infrastructure.

WHO and WHO Patient Safety. 2009. A Guide to the Implementation of the WHO Multimodal Hand Hygiene Improvement Strategy.